Dru

in the South-West?

Paul White

Bossiney Books

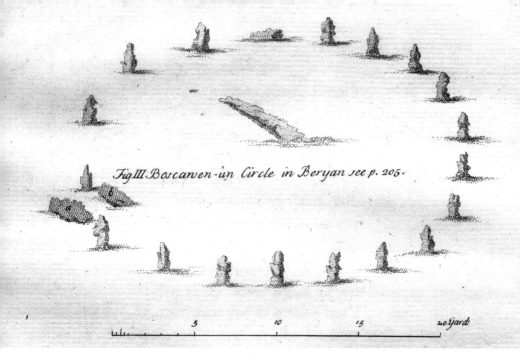

Boscawen-un, one of many meticulously sketched illustrations in Borlase's 'Antiquities of Cornwall'

Front cover: The Cheesewring (which Borlase calls the Wringcheese) near Minions on Bodmin Moor

Title page: 'A peep into the Sanctum Sanctorum, 6 June 1724', from William Stukeley's 'Stonehenge, a Work of the British Druids Described'

By the same author: *Ancient Dartmoor*

First published 2017 by Bossiney Books Ltd
33 Queens Drive, Ilkley, LS29 9QW
www.bossineybooks.com
ISBN 978-1-906474-65-2

Acknowledgements
The author and publishers are grateful to the Leeds Library and the Yorkshire Archaeological & Historical Society for permission to photograph historic books in their collections.
Printed in Great Britain by R Booth Ltd, Penryn, Cornwall

Introduction

A year or so ago in a moment of extravagance I purchased a copy of the Revd William Borlase's *Antiquities of Cornwall* in its sumptuously illustrated 1769 second edition, and was fascinated to read the author's opinion that stone circles, chamber tombs ('quoits') and even granite outcrops such as the Cheesewring should be attributed to the druids, who seemed to be everywhere in Cornwall:

> The town of Redruth was anciently called Red-drew, or more rightly Ryd-drew, i.e. the Druids ford or crossing of the brook…

> The rock now called the Wringcheese is a group of rocks that attracts the admiration of all travellers… It may seem to some that this is an artificial building of flat stones layed carefully on one another, and raised to this height by human skill and labour; but as there are several heaps of stones on the same hill, and also on a hill about a mile distant called Kell-mar'r, of like fabric too, though not near so high as this, I should think it a natural crag, and that what stones surrounded it and hid its grandeur, were removed by the Druids. From its having rock basons, from the uppermost stone's being a rocking-stone, and the great elevation of this group, I think we may truly reckon it among the rock-deities, and that its tallness and just balance might probably be intended to express the stateliness and justice of the supreme being. Secondly, as the rock-basons show that it was usual to get upon the top of this karn, it might probably serve for the Druid to harangue the audience, pronounce decisions, and foretell future events.

And Borlase, a leading antiquary of his day, was by no means alone. From about 1720 to about 1860, antiquaries became convinced that these stone monuments were constructed as temples of 'the druids'. Many antiquaries were also clergymen, and they were fascinated by what the druids might have believed. Their conjectures became ever more extraordinary, expanding from a tiny amount of evidence in classical sources. The druids were imagined in various

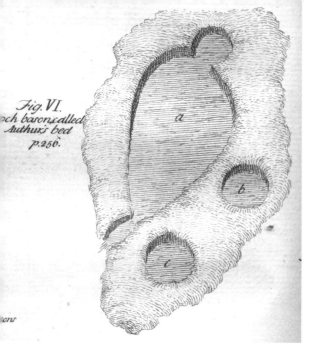

Fig. VI.
ch bason called
Authur's bed
p.250.

ens

A rock basin (or bason)
illustrated by Borlase.
These natural features
lie on top of most granite
rocks, but were fantasised as
druidic carvings, made to
receive sacrificial blood, or
for divination purposes.

forms to suit the writer's prejudices: they might be wise mono-theists who welcomed Christianity, or devils incarnate who delighted in human gore.

This short book is an attempt to understand both how and why these men got it so wrong, and how we came gradually to recognise the antiquity of the stone monuments which are so common in the South-West, especially on Dartmoor and in West Penwith, as well as the huge constructions further east, at Stanton Drew, Avebury and Stonehenge. These monuments are now dated to various peri-ods from about 4500 BC to about 1500 BC, rather than to the time of the druids, around 100 BC.

So this book will cover the history of the concept of 'prehistory' – a word first coined in 1851, just as archaeology began to take on its modern form.

But the study of prehistory was a specialist antiquarian interest. In the later eighteenth century the idea of 'druids' spread much more widely, entering the popular imagination, and in the Romantic period became a staple subject of Gothic poetry and fiction, even of Italian opera – Bellini's *Norma*.

Druid hermitages and statues of druids could soon be found

sprouting up in landscaped gardens, and they were an element in Romantic tourism. Richard Polwhele, a less than meticulous historian of Devon, wrote:

> The Valley of Stones [the Valley of the Rocks at Lynton] in the vicinity of Exmoor, is so awfully magnificent, that we need not hesitate in pronouncing it to have been the favourite residence of Druidism

while admitting that there isn't the faintest shred of evidence for it. Polwhele also wrote verse, for example, in 1781:

> Yet, where the lurid nightshade blooms,
> To some lone ruin's deep'ning glooms
> The pensive poet steals:
> Oft as he marks the Druid graves
> And crumbling piles, his bosom heaves
> With thoughts of ancient days, and pleasing horror feels!

Even more strangely, various groups decided to call themselves druids, from quasi-masonic societies to 'modern pagans'. Being unable to understand why anyone would wish to connect their own beliefs with a semi-mythological antiquity, I have not spent much time researching this aspect – despite being intrigued to find a photograph of Winston Churchill's initiation as a druid in 1908.

In nineteenth century Wales, imaginary druids were fused with the real bardic tradition, assisted by the forgeries of Iolo Morganwg, and became part of Welsh cultural nationalism. It is astonishing to find the *Rough Guide to Wales*, 2015 edition, saying:

> … while stone circles, intricately carved monoliths and finely balanced capstones set at crucial points on ancient pathways suggest the more spiritual life led by the priestly druids.

Clearly the archaeological message has not yet got across!

What evidence was there?

Very little. There are two groups of Greek and Roman sources, and the relevant quotations in their entirety would probably fit into a dozen pages. The first group consists primarily of Julius Caesar writing c. 50 BC, Pliny the Elder c. AD 70 (he died in the eruption of Vesuvius in AD 79) and Tacitus a generation later.

The second group is of less interest today, as they wrote centuries after the extermination of the druids, and were in many cases involved in theological speculation, for example about the hypothetical common origin of the druid and Brahmin religions – but this was a subject which fascinated some writers in the 17th and 18th centuries.

Caesar (see page 37) wrote about the druids in Gaul, and said that 'It is thought that the discipline originated in Britain and was then brought into Gaul, and nowadays those who are particularly keen to understand it generally head there for further education.'

But curiously, when Caesar describes his two unsuccessful forays into Britain he makes no mention of druids. It should be remembered that Caesar was not an unbiased author. He was writing up his own achievements while ruthlessly angling for supreme power, and what he has to say about Britain, or indeed Gaul, has to be assessed as something written by a devious politician.

Tacitus in the *Annals* described an attack in AD 60 by the Roman army against Mona, now accepted as Anglesey, 'an island strong in its inhabitants and a haven for refugees':

> On the shore stood a varied line of battle, dense with armed men with women running among them, dressed in funeral clothes like the Furies and with hair dishevelled, waving burning brands. And the druids all around, pouring out dreadful curses, lifting their hands up to heaven, unnerved the soldiers by the novelty of the sight, so that their limbs were paralysed and they were like sitting ducks. Then, pulling themselves together by their general's encouragement not to be scared of a flurry of crazy women, they carried the standards forward and overthrew those in their way, wrapping them up in their own fiery brands.
>
> A force was then imposed on the conquered, and the groves destroyed which were sacred to savage superstitions – for they held it as divine law that they should cover their altars with the blood of captives and consult the gods by studying human entrails.

Yet when Tacitus wrote a biography of his father-in-law Agricola, he made no mention of druids, though Agricola had been a young officer in Britain at the time of the attack on Anglesey, and in AD 77 was given supreme command of the Roman army in Britain, where he completed the conquest of Wales.

Nowhere does Tacitus, or any other writer, suggest that Mona was a druidic centre, just their last refuge.

The elder Pliny had served as an officer and then as an administrator in various provinces, but not in Britain or Gaul, and in any case the druids were by his time a thing of the past. In his encyclopaedic *Natural History* (page 39), he tells us that the Gaulish druids ('for that is the name they give to their magicians') 'held nothing more sacred than the mistletoe and the tree that bears it, supposing always that tree to be the robur [*Quercus robur*, the pedunculate oak].' He describes a ritual where a priest cuts the mistletoe with a golden sickle before bulls are sacrificed:

> It is the belief with them that the mistletoe, taken in drink,

will impart fecundity to all animals that are barren, and that it is an antidote for all poisons. Such are the religious feelings which we find entertained towards trifling objects among nearly all nations.

Pliny is the only primary source for the connection between druids and oak trees. He had little respect for the druids, but in any case he is hardly a reliable authority, being somewhat credulous, as is apparent from the inclusion in his encyclopaedia of men with only one leg, which they could use to shade themselves from the midday sun. The illustration below is from an equally credulous *Book of Prodigies* by the 4th century Julius Obsequens, reconstructed in an illustrated edition of 1552, with a reference to Pliny.

A comprehensive summary of the unreliability of the classical sources can be found in Ronald Hutton's *Blood and Mistletoe*, Yale University Press 2009.

De prodiis

10

Scipodes.
Monomeri.

Cathaini.

SCipodes & Monomeri gentes, qui unum tātum pedē habentes, non flecten- tes poplitem, mirabilis cele- ritatis. Hi Plinio teste per æ- stiuum tempus, in terra su- pini iacentes, pedum se um- bra protegunt.

CAthaini inter Gedro- siam, atq̃ Indum fluui- um, Scythicum genus ho- minū, qui aiunt se solos ho- minum duobus luminibus cernere, cæteros mortales aūt aut cæcos esse, aut altero oculo captos. Candidum genus hominum, paruis oculis, natu- ra imberbes, uerępietatis omnino ex pertes, solem & lunam adorant, fusi les statuas, nonnulli bouem.

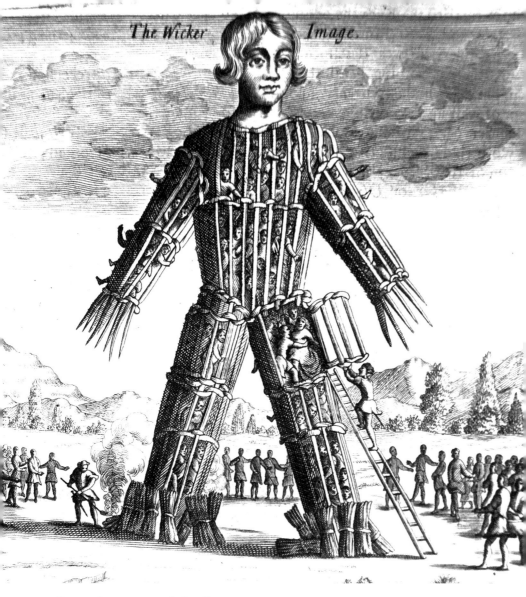

Stonehenge and Avebury

Whilst druids had featured in poetry and on the stage in the 17th century, and Aylett Sammes in his *Britannia Antiqua Illustrata* (1676) had provided the archetypal illustration of a druid, and a magnificently imaginative wicker man (above), the great debate about whether the druids were responsible for the stone monuments of the British Isles centred on Stonehenge and Avebury.

The archetypal druid, as first pictured by Aylett Sammes, 1676, rather strangely holding a book

John Aubrey

The first person to suggest that Stonehenge dated from the time of the druids, and the 'discoverer' of Avebury, was John Aubrey (1627-1697), a Wiltshire gentleman. His life was something of a mess – his university studies interrupted by the Civil Wars, inheriting debts from his father, being a financial muddler, getting himself expensively sued for breach of promise, and ultimately living as a bankrupt dependent on his many, many friends.

He was however a great gatherer of information – antiquarian, scientific, folklore, whatever came his way. Unfortunately he was no more able to get the information in order and publish it than he was to run his family estates, but he did come up with splendid ideas: perhaps the centre of the earth is a massive fire, which causes volcanic activity? Perhaps it would be possible to discover the age of a building by comparing the style of its windows and arches with other buildings, of known date? Perhaps we could do the same with handwriting styles and historic costume? He also wrote, 'The world is much older than is commonly supposed.'

Whilst out hunting with friends in January 1649, Aubrey suddenly recognised the huge stone circle at Avebury as an ancient structure:

> This old monument does as much excel in bignes the so renowned Stoneheng, as a cathedral doeth a parish church: so that by the grandure one might presume it to have been an Arch-temple of the Druids.

Before long he had revisited the site and mapped it, one of the very first archaeological field surveys. Much later, he brought it to the attention of King Charles II.

He made similar surveys of Stonehenge, and was the first to suggest that Stonehenge was a druid temple. At the time, that was a perceptive statement, not an idiocy. To understand why, here is an extract from the 1695 edition of Camden's *Britannia*, a meticulously scholarly revision by Edmund Gibson of the most influential historical work of the previous century:

> This celebrated piece of antiquity [Stonehenge] hath engaged the pens of several curious and learned persons; and almost as many as have written, have fallen into several and distinct opinions concerning the occasion and antiquity of it.
>
> Which opinions, with some few remarks upon them, it may not be improper to subjoin; and such a short view, is all that the nature of our present design will admit. The opinions about it may be reduc'd to these 7 heads:
>
> 1. That it is a work of the Phœnicians, as Mr. Sammes in his *Britannia* conceits; a conjecture, that has met with so little approbation, that I shall not stay to confute it.
>
> 2. That it was a Temple of the Druids long before the coming-in of the Romans; which Mr. John Aubrey, Fellow of the Royal Society, endeavours to prove in his manuscript treatise, entitled *Monumenta Britannica*.

3. That it was an old triumphal British monument, erected to Anaraith the Goddess of Victory, after a bloody battle won by the illustrious Stanings and his Cangick Giants, against Divitiacus and his Belgæ; and that the captives and spoils were sacrificed to the said idol in this temple. An opinion advanced (upon what grounds I know not) in an anonymous MS. written about the year 1666.

4. That it was a monument rais'd by the Britains in memory of Queen Boadicia; which is advanced by the author of *Nero-Caesar*. [Edmund Bolton]

5. That it was a temple, built by the Romans to the god Cœlum or Terminus, of the Tuscan order; which is Mr. Jones's opinion in his ingenious conjectures upon this subject.

6. That it was the burial-place of Uther Pendragon, Constantine, Ambrosius, and other British Kings; or, as others would have it, a monument set-up by Ambrosius in memory of the Britains slain here.

7. That it was a Danish monument, erected either for a burial-place, or as a trophy for some victory, or for the election and coronation of their kings.

The two dominant explanations of the day were that Stonehenge was a Danish structure, because a Danish writer named Ole Worm had shown there were similar structures in Scandinavia, and the theory of James I's court architect Inigo Jones that it was Roman. To be fair, Jones was probably less than fully convinced of this, because he never published his ideas: it was left to his son-in-law to do so after his death, with great zeal, in 1655.

Scottish druids

Whilst Aubrey was probably the first to associate Stonehenge with the druids, a Paris-based Scot, Hector Boece (1465-1536), had suggested in 1526 that druids had constructed stone circles near Aberdeen – and Aubrey had read Boece.

An inward View of STONEHENGE ·AA *the altar.*
or Side view of the cell.

An engraving made from one of Stukeley's many sketches, mostly drawn in 1724, well before he published his book about Stonehenge

Aubrey was merely saying that it was a pre-Roman construction by the Ancient Britons, of a religious rather than a sepulchral nature, and that since the priests of the Ancient Britons were called druids, Stonehenge was a temple of the druids. Edmund Gibson does not commit himself on which of the seven theories is right, but rather inclines to the view that it is a work of the Ancient Britons, but constructed after they have seen the architecture of the Romans, and learned a bit from it.

William Stukeley

As a young man, Stukeley was lent a copy of Aubrey's manuscript notes on Avebury and Stonehenge, and followed them up with visits to both places. Whereas Aubrey resisted the temptation to take holy orders and a comfortable living, despite his financial problems, Stukeley surprised his deist friends by becoming a priest.

Deists theoretically believed in a God, but did not subscribe to any Christian sect: in practice they were quite varied, from out-right atheists concealing their total lack of belief in order to avoid persecution, to believers in an original religion revealed by God to Adam, of which all surviving religions were descendants which had fallen into various degrees of error.

Stukeley was probably one of the latter, believing the druids to have been a Good Thing, whereas a deist friend, John Toland, believed they were hypocritical charlatans, just as he perceived the priests of the established church to be. Stukeley wrote to Borlase:

> All my studies in antiquity have ever had a regard to religion. Nor do I think any other studies are worth cultivating, but what have some aspect that way.

In 1740, Stukeley published a superbly illustrated folio volume entitled *Stonehenge, a Work of the British Druids Described*. This book probably influenced thinking about druids more widely than any other. The description and plans both of Stonehenge and Avebury were mostly of high quality, though Stukeley's wilder theories about the beliefs of his monotheistic druids were smiled at by other antiquaries, and his preconception that there was a serpent motif at these sites made him misinterpret the evidence.

A side elevation of Stonehenge by Stukeley, who was convinced the builders had measured in 'druid cubits'

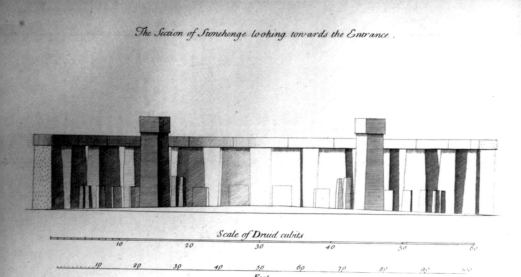

The Section of Stonehenge looking towards the Entrance.

Scale of Druid cubits
10   20   30   40   50   60

10   20   30   40   50   60   70   80   90
Feet

Prejudices and temptations

Antiquaries, and particularly clergymen, were often trying to fit their discoveries into an existing theory; misinterpreting evidence, and even misrepresenting it, was all too common. There were a number of factors.

One problem was a literal belief in the *Book of Genesis*. Various attempts had been made to calculate the exact date of the Creation and of the Flood, and Bishop Ussher's version was to prevail, with Creation in 4004 BC (some time after 6 pm on Saturday 22 October) and the Flood in 2348 BC. After the Flood, Noah's sons departed in different directions to populate the world, and whilst the date on which their descendants reached the white cliffs of Dover was not known for certain, it was fairly clear that it could not have been more than a few hundred years before the Romans came.

With that mindset, there was no room for multiple ancient British cultures. If the druids were the priests of the ancient Britons, then they must have already been around when the earliest pre-Roman monuments were built. And since *Genesis* was the history of the world from its creation, dictated by a particularly reliable author (though unfortunately he had not given much detail about the British Isles), there could be no such thing as 'pre-history'.

Protestantism and patriotism also combined to affect wishful thinking. If the British druids were indeed monotheists who had readily accepted Christianity in the second century AD, then the foundation of the British church preceded the arrival of the Romist St Augustine, giving the Church of England precedence over the usurping Roman Catholics. And it was very reassuring that the ancient Britons, urged on by their druid priests, had presented such a powerful resistance to the Romans: clearly they were patriots to be highly esteemed.

The Union of England and Wales with Scotland in 1707 led to a greater acceptance of the story of the ancient Britons as part of the history of the new nation. Through the 18th century this acceptance of 'Celtic' culture steadily grew: the works of Ossian

Opposite: Stukeley's 'Stonehenge' includes this esoteric genealogy of the descendants of Noah

Left: Just how primitive were the ancient Britons? This illustration was by John Speed in 1611, and was probably influenced by pictures of the native people of Virginia

(substantially adapted, if not invented, by his 'translator' James Macpherson) were warmly welcomed in England as well as Scotland, as forming part of a collective British historical culture which made us distinct from the rest of Europe.

At the same time, from the late Elizabethan period British explorers and traders had encountered 'primitive' people, firstly the native Americans, then in the late 18th century the Pacific islanders. The attitudes both of those with direct experience, and those at home who read about the encounters, were decidedly ambiguous. Were these people disgustingly barbaric, or were they 'the noble

The GENEALOGY.

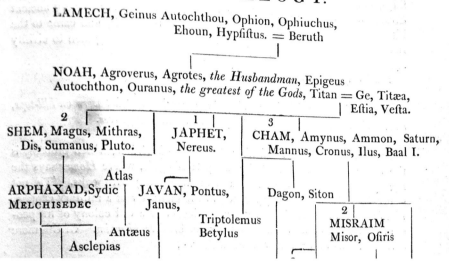

savage'? Were the ancient Britons as primitive as these people?

If so, surely they could not have built Stonehenge?

And – the other side of the coin – how were the Romans to be seen, when compared with growing British imperial ambitions? Were they just greedy invaders, or were they admirable for spreading civilisation?

And had Caesar, Pliny and Tacitus created for their own purposes a false impression of the 'primitive' societies of ancient Britain? To which the answer, then as now, was, almost certainly yes.

Then there was room within the 'Celtic' societies of the Scottish Highlands, Wales and Ireland for a whole range of different perceptions of these questions. All these factors led to a wide range of what the archaeologist Stuart Piggott described as 'druids-as-wished-for'.

The techniques available to antiquaries were very limited. Once they were beyond the reach of classical texts, they were primarily dependent on manuscripts and coins which had been found. But there were no pre-Roman British manuscripts, and precious few coins. They were reduced to using conjecture, the wildly misleading techniques of etymology, and assumptions that things known (or thought to be known) about other parts of the ancient world were also relevant to Britain. With these methods, the wildest fantasies could be presented as reality.

More antiquaries

Henry Rowlands

Another book which influenced antiquarian thinking about the druids was *Mona Antiqua Restaurata: An Archaeological Discourse on the Antiquities, Natural and Historical, of the Isle of Anglesey, the Antient Seat of the British Druids*, by Henry Rowlands (1655-1723), a clergyman based on Anglesey, who died just before publication. Rowlands totally misinterpreted Tacitus, who merely says Anglesey was the last refuge of the druids, and determined that the island had been the centre of British druidry.

That idea took root, and became an article of Welsh patriotic faith: the *Rough Guide*, quoted earlier, still believes it.

John Wood the Elder

John Wood was the architect for much of Bath, including the Circus. The atmosphere he created there seems reposed, classical, rational. But just consider the giant acorn finials that adorn the parapet. Acorns, oak trees, druids… The plan of the Circus is based on a masonic symbol, and the measurements are those of Stonehenge, of which Wood had made an extremely accurate plan.

Wood had some strange ideas, which can be found in his books (on-line as are many of the sources referred to) *An Essay towards a description of the City of Bath* (1742) and *Choir Gaure, vulgarly called Stonehenge on Salisbury Plain, Described, Restored, and Explained* (1747). (*Choir Gaure* was an old name for Stonehenge, meaning 'Circle-dance of the giants'.) For example:

> Druidism immediately spread itself from Britain eastward to the utmost corners of the earth, instead of coming from the extremity of the eastern world to us. The Indian Hylobii seem therefore to have had their rise from the British Druids; and the learning of the latter seems to have soon reached China itself, Confucius rising up in that country and appearing as a great philosopher at the head of four orders of priests about thirty years after the death of Pythagoras.

But he could be even more idiosyncratic:

> The monuments of antiquity immediately surrounding the hot springs of Bath, consecrated in the times of paganism to the Sun, appeared to me, when considered collectively, to be the remains of the metropolitan seat of such a learned set of priests; and the Saxon name having been Achmanchester, that is, the Oak Men's City; and the existence, the heat, and the virtues of the waters of the Sun having been attributed to the magical art, very much confirmed me in my ideas; other monuments of antiquity lying by the side of a river, about eight miles westward of the hot springs, seemed to be the ruins of the university, or great school of learning of the same sect of priests; since Stantondrew, the name of the village in which they are situated, imports the Oak Men's Town, built with stone...
>
> The great resemblance, and the manifest connection which appears to have been, between the works of Bath, or the city of the oak men, and those of Stanton-Drew, or the town of oak men, makes it more than probable that all those works were founded by one and the same person,

and for the same purposes, to wit, to honour the gods, to cure the diseases of the people, and to instruct them in the liberal sciences. For these oak men, like Zoroastres and his disciples in Persia, had their cave too, which is to this day called Okey-Hole, and is situated by Wells…

Bladud caused the works of Stanton-Drew to be made… this circle made the college of an high priest, and four priests of an inferior order, at the same time that it represented the earth in the model of the planetary system… These priests were, in general, called Druids.

Naturally East Harptree, a village on the north side of the Mendips, must have been 'where the poets exercised the functions assigned to them by their institution; and more particularly where they played upon their harps, and to those musical instruments, sang their melodious songs'.

Don't let this insanity deter you from visiting both Bath and the splendid stone circle at Stanton Drew!

William Borlase (1696-1772)

Borlase was born in Pendeen, educated at Oxford, then went straight back to Cornwall as Rector of Lugvan and later simultaneously Vicar of St Just. He actively sought out Methodist preachers and had them press-ganged into the Navy: John Wesley only narrowly missed this treatment! Apart from his *Antiquities of Cornwall*, he published a study of the Isles of Scilly and a *Natural History of Cornwall*.

The *Antiquities* was well received (though as is the case with most of these authors, the number of copies of an expensive book sold was extremely limited) and other remote areas of the British Isles soon received comparable attention. In some ways Borlase was trying to be cautious:

In treating of the superstition and rock-monuments of the Druids, I may seem too conjectural to those who will make no allowances for the deficiencies of history, nor be satisfied with anything but evident truths; but where there

A view of Avebury, by Stukeley

is no certainty to be obtained, probabilities must suffice;
and conjectures are no faults, but when they are either
advanced as real truths, or too copiously pursued, or
peremptorily insisted upon as decisive. In subjects of such
distant ages, where History will so often withdraw her
taper, Conjecture may sometimes strike a new light...

In 1785 Edward Ledwich, in an article in the journal of the
Society of Antiquaries of London, *Archaeologia*, produced a devas-
tating critique of conjecture:

Give a date and a name, and a man of leisure and letters
will, almost instantly, create a piece of history or chronology, seemingly regular and consistent; and by this means of
conjectures, by straining passages and combining the most
heterogeneous, and by various other arts of literary
pharmacy... events have been settled; history ascertained
and manners described, that never existed beyond the
author's imagination. The popular voice gives a temporary

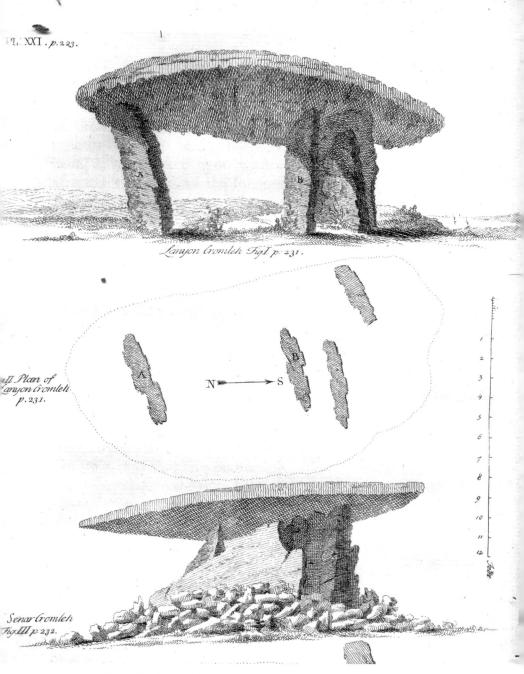

Lanyon Cromleh Fig I p. 231.

II. Plan of Lanyon Cromleh p. 231.

Senar Cromleh Fig III p. 232.

A study by Borlase of Lanyon and Zennor Quoits. Such studies can still be useful when a monument has been subsequently damaged and badly repaired, as at Lanyon

merit to such productions: reason at length recovers from her delirium, and we are then ashamed to find the object of our admiration to have been some groundless hypothesis or historical Romance… On no subject has fancy roamed with more licentious indulgence than on that of the Druids and their institutions.

But it would be another seventy years before reason recovered from her druidic delirium!

Richard Polwhele

Certainly Revd Richard Polwhele (1760-1838) was still deluded in the 1790s in his account of Devon, where he believed the druids had arrived from the Middle East:

> That Druidism then, as originally existing in Devonshire and Cornwall, was immediately transported, in all its purity and perfection, from the east, seems to me extremely probable.

At least that was less unlikely than John Wood's idea of Confucianism as a British export.

One Devon monument had become well known before anything on Dartmoor, the 'Drewsteignton cromlech' now known as Spinster's Rock. Polwhele correctly takes to task a certain Mr Chapple, who had argued that it was an astronomical observatory (an idea much older than you might expect) but does so with rather antiquated rhetoric:

> I would as soon believe that the earth was formed by a concourse of atoms, as that four rude and shapeless stones, to all appearance selected only for their magnitude, should exhibit an exact correspondence with every circle in the heavens.

Polwhele inevitably derived 'Drewsteignton' from 'the town of the Druids upon the Teign', and wrote that it 'seems to have been singled out by the Druids, as the peculiar seat of their religion'; needless to say, he was wrong!

Druids and tourists

Whilst Polwhele in his Devon histories seems almost to have been writing with tourists in mind, and there certainly were some visitors in his day, earlier visitors had made no mention of druids. For example, Samuel Pepys had visited Wiltshire in 1668:

> So [leaving] the three women behind W.H. Murfd. and our guide, and I single, to Stonehege [sic] over the plain and some prodigious great hills even to fright us. Came thither and find them as prodigious as any tale I ever heard of them and worth going this journey to see. God knows what their use was. They are hard to tell but yet may be told.
>
> Gave the shepherd woman for leading our horses, 4^d.

Not a druid in sight, there or at Avebury. Only from the 1760s do published tours and then guide books begin to mention sites as 'druidic'. Benjamin Donn's one-inch-to-the-mile map of Devon published in 1765 shows Spinster's Rock as 'A Druid Cromleh', as well as a nearby 'Moving Stone', which was a logan stone which lay (indeed still lies) in the Teign, and which reputedly rocked in the past – Polwhele claims he 'easily rock'd it with one hand… it was, probably, balanced with such nicety in former times, as to move with the slightest touch'.

But Spinster's Rock seems to be the only megalith noticed in Devon. Within the West Country, perhaps a few visitors to Bath went to Stanton Drew, travellers along the old route of the A30 might divert to Drewsteignton, and the occasional visitor to Cornwall gets as far as Boscawen-un, but it is not until around 1820 that serious interest is taken, and nobody seems to have noted Dartmoor's monuments until even later. Samuel Rowe in 1848 recalls:

> Those curious relics of the aboriginal period of our history, the stone avenues, had attracted little notice, and indeed had been scarcely mentioned by our local topographers or antiquaries, before our examination of those near Merivale [sic] bridge in the year 1827.

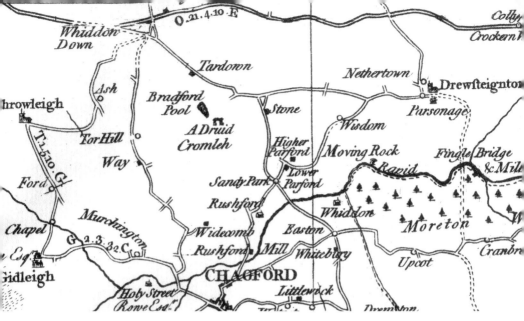

Spinsters' Rock as a Druid Cromleh in Benjamin Donn's map, 1765

The Revd John Bathurst Deane in *The Worship of the Serpent traced throughout the World* (1833), after noting Merrivale comments:

> Other monuments of the same nature are scattered over Dartmoor, which from the multitude of such and similar British remains must have been very thickly inhabited.

But the most passionate exponent of Dartmoor's druidic past is 'Mrs Bray' in *A description of the part of Devonshire bordering on the Tamar and the Tavy* (1836). The very names of the tors reflected the names of the gods of the druids:

> God of battles, *Hesus* so Hessary Tor
> Belus or *Bel*, the sun god, so Bel Tor
> *Ham*, a British god, so Ham Tor
>
> … and my venerable and learned friend, the Revd Mr Polwhele, in his *History of Devon*, refers to the worship of that deity all the numerous Hams of this county. [!!!]
>
> … on the moor, the Druid moved in the region of the vast and the sublime: the rocks, the winter torrent, the distant and expanded ocean, the works of the great God of nature, in their simplest and in their most imposing character, were

25

A.

B

C

A Druid seat of Judgment.

Carn Brea, with an imagined 'Seat of Judgement' from which the druid as supreme Justice of the Peace could deliver his verdict

all before his view.

Anna Eliza Bray (1790-1883), a popular historical novelist, was the wife of Revd Edward Atkyns Bray, vicar of Tavistock where he had been born in 1778. He purchased Beardown Farm.

> My husband considers Bair-down to have been the hill of bards… Should it be thought he is incorrect in his view of the original claims of the hill to a bardic character, he has now at least fully established them, by the inscriptions on the granite with which he has partly covered several of those enormous masses that arise, with so much magnificence, in the midst of the River Cowsic, that flows at the foot of the eminence on which the house was built by his father… he used to paint the inscriptions himself, in large characters, upon the rocks, and then employ a labourer with what is here called a pick to work them out. Some of these inscriptions were in triads, and engraved on the rocks in the bardic character of the sprig alphabet, as it is given by the Revd Edward Davies in his Celtic Remains. [She means Edward Davies' *Celtic Researches*.]

> [My husband] gave the name Mona to one of the mini-islands in the Cowsic, and composed the following inscription:

> > Ye tuneful birds! ye Druids of the grove!
> > Who sing not strains of blood, but lays of love,
> > To whom this Isle, a little Mona's given –
> > Ne'er from the sacred spot shall ye be driven.

> These rugged rocks, last barrier to the skies,
> Smoked with the Druids' secret sacrifice;
> Alas! blind man, to hope with human blood
> To please a God, all merciful and good.

On one occasion, the tenant farmer at Beardown, John Hannaford, took the Brays to Wistmans Wood:

> The farmer, Hannaford, is our guide... the farmer says, "'Tis a wisht old place, sure enough, and full of adders as can be."
>
> This last communication somewhat cools my enthusiasm about Druid groves; but the farmer offers and supplies a speedy remedy – one, too, of most mystical origin, and not a little heathenish, being derived from the very Druids upon whose haunts we are about to intrude; for he transfers to my hand the ashen bough or sprig that he was carrying in his own, and initiates me on the spot into the pagan rites of charming adders, to render them harmless as the poorest worm that crawls upon the earth. He tells me, that the moment I see an adder I have nothing to do but draw a circle with an ash rod round it, and that the creature will never go out of it; nay, if a fire were kindled in the ring, it would rather go into the fire itself than pass the circle...
>
> Now all these things considered induce me to believe that as Dartmoor must from the earliest times have been most prolific in vipers, the mode of charming them with an ashen wand, still retained by the peasantry of the moor, is nothing less than a vestige of the customs of Druid antiquity.

Merrivale is certainly not ignored, indeed it becomes a 'Cursus or Via Sacra, used for processions, chariot races, &c., and in the Druidical Ceremonies'. She has been assimilating the recent Welsh pseudo-scholarship (see page 31):

> According to Davies, the sacred ship of glass was borne along the cursus with the utmost pomp on the day of observing the mysteries of the Helio-arkite god. The

View of the Cell of the Celtic Temple at Abury. Aug.ᵗ 16. 1721

The Cove of the Northern temple.

Another view of Avebury by Stukeley: much of the monument was subsequently destroyed for its stone

procession of Godo, the British Ceres, was no less splendid: it took place in the evening, as that of the solar deity did in the morning. And the cursors at that moment must have presented scenes like those exhibited by the abominable priests of Baal, of whom we read in the Bible: for in the midst of their wild dances, they cut and lacerated their bodies in honour of her mystic rites. 'Let the thigh be pierced with blood,' says Taliesin…

I shall never visit that spot without indulging one of those day-dreams of romance that are so truly delightful. I shall fancy white-robed Druids, and blue-robed bards…

The full gushings of Mrs Bray can be found online, and are heartily recommended, if you have an idle moment.

The demise of the druids

When did all this nonsense end? Well, in popular culture perhaps it never did! But among the highly educated, the end came quite suddenly, around 1850-60. One major advance was the 'three age system', which had been proposed in Denmark in 1831, the idea that the Stone Age was followed by the Bronze Age and then by the Iron Age. Caesar's druids belong in the Iron Age. British antiquaries were slow to take up this chronology, though Sir John Lubbock developed it in 1865 by subdividing the Stone Age into Palaeolithic and Neolithic.

It is tempting to say that 1859 was the year things changed in Britain, because that was the year of two events which altered attitudes in the scholarly world. The first is well known, the publication by Darwin of *On the Origin of Species*. The second, much less well known, occurred in Devon. William Pengelly, a self-educated geologist and archaeologist born in Cornwall, excavated a newly discovered cave at Brixham using for the first time a novel scientific method – stratigraphy. He was able to give proofs of the antiquity of mankind.

The publicity generated by these two events seems to have broken barriers of caution which had prevailed. Many people with scientific interests (there were as yet few professional scientists) had been reluctant to incur the wrath of the religious community – especially if they were clergymen themselves. Suddenly they were free to say what they thought, and discuss new ideas.

The change was rapidly picked up by the publishers of popular guidebooks. Whereas the 1856 edition of *Murray's Handbook for Travellers in Devon and Cornwall* quoted Borlase enthusiastically, and referred to:

> sacred circles, or Druidical circles as they are commonly called… There can be little doubt that these venerable relics were the hypaethral temples of our Druidic forefathers.

in the 1872 edition the editor clearly states:

> … the tourist should be especially warned against all
> such theories as connect the cromlechs and stone circles

It was not only the druids who disappeared. This magnificent logan stone was the Tolmen at Constantine, and was in fact balanced on just one of the supports. The rock was exploded off its perch in 1869, and broken up for its high quality granite. Antiquaries tried to prevent this kind of desctruction but were not always successful.

with Druidism, and its supposed rites. The rites and the 'Druidism' are in most cases as shadowy and unreal as the theories which have been founded on them; and it will be well to remember that a thorough examination of the remains themselves, and a careful comparison of them with similar relics existing in other parts of the world, are the only means by which we can hope to arrive at any certain knowledge of their origin.

But the book's unfortunate editor was clearly instructed to refer favourably to another book published by Murray that year, James Fergusson's *Rude Stone Monuments*. He does so with some embarassment and contorted prose, because Fergusson is convinced that Stonehenge was built after the departure of the Romans!

Druid popularity and the Celtic Revival

The attitudes of people like Polwhele and Mrs Bray were greatly influenced by two major cultural trends, Romanticism and the Celtic Revival. The period of extreme enthusiasm for druids was 1750-1850, broadly contemporaneous with these. In Britain 'Romantic' attitudes to landscape developed from an earlier interest in the 'sublime' and the 'picturesque'. A passion for Nature was central to the aesthetics of Romanticism, and the druids, widely seen as supremely wise priests of nature and famous for worshipping in sacred groves, fitted very well into this picture.

A strange offshoot of Romanticism was 'Gothic' fiction, satirised in Jane Austen's *Northanger Abbey*, where the reader could experience a pleasurable kind of terror – and druids could help here too, if you accepted their enthusiasm for human sacrifice.

During the second half of the 18th century – once the uprising of 1745 had faded into the background and the southern Scots and the English felt more secure – there was an ever increasing interest in Scottish Highland culture, which culminated in the huge popularity of Sir Walter Scott, the invention of clan tartans and Queen Victoria's private purchase of Balmoral. Druids scarcely featured in this process, but it was quite a different matter in Wales.

The Welsh had a genuine bardic tradition, often with a hereditary element, and there was a very substantial body of Welsh language literature which had been preserved in manuscript. The number of such manuscripts greatly increased as a result of the activities of the antiquary Edward Williams (1747-1826), a fascinating character better known by his bardic name Iolo Morganwg. Alas, a more complete account of him would be out of place in this book!

Iolo insisted that a Welsh druidic (as well as bardic) tradition had survived Roman persecution, conversion to Christianity and the efforts of Edward I to suppress the bards. Later it became clear that he had forged his 'new discoveries', both by creating original material and by adapting genuine manuscripts. In his lifetime his forgeries were widely accepted, with unfortunate effects for some genuine Welsh scholars, including Edward 'Celtic' Davies.

The traditional druid here drawn by Stukeley, in close imitation of that by Aylett Sammes – but without a book. Most 'druidic' ceremonial dress is based on this, but usually with more consideration for chilly knees

It was while living in London that Iolo Morganwg founded the Gorsedd Beirdd Ynys Prydain (Gorsedd of Bards of the Island of Britain) with rituals supposedly based on ancient druidry. The first of these events was held at the unlikely north London venue of Primrose Hill in 1792. The annual Gorsedd continues to be very important, to Welsh speakers particularly: it is non-religious, aiming to celebrate achievements not least in literature; its membership includes the former Archbishop of Canterbury Rowan Williams.

There is a comparable Gorsedh Kernow which meets annually in Cornwall; it is bardic rather than druidic, but has been known to meet within stone circles. The robes worn at these meetings are of a distinctively druidic style.

Modern druids

The appeal of the druids soon made some people want to emulate them, but in various ways. The fact that the ancient druids had, according to Caesar, been one half of the Gaulish (and presumably the British) elite made them acceptable to the British upper clases.

Exactly what the members of 'modern' druid societies were told about 'ancient mysteries', how much of the mumbo jumbo they believed, and whether they had ulterior social motives, is impossible to know: in the eighteenth and nineteenth centuries the 'druidic' societies seem to have appealed to the same kinds of men as did the masons.

William Stukeley, briefly an enthusiastic mason, founded a quasi-masonic Society of Roman Knights, and gave himself the name of a Gaulish druid, Chyndonax. He liked to be called 'the Druid'.

The Druidical Society of Anglesey was founded in 1772, and lasted till 1844. It was composed mainly of the social elite of the island, and its purpose was charitable, for example supporting a hospital in Liverpool. A 'Druids of Cardigan' society on the other hand was an excuse for poetry and picnics. The Ancient Order of Druids was formed in London in 1781, and concentrated on performing music: politics and religion were both taboo subjects. By 1831 it had 193 Lodges, but two years later half the membership left to form a more democratically run United Ancient Order of Druids. Both flourished. None of these groups looked to the ancient druids for spiritual inspiration.

In fact these and other 'druid' societies were often co-operative 'friendly societies' for working men, with members contributing regularly to an insurance fund from which they could draw in case of financial misfortune. In their day they had hundreds of thousands of members, not just in Britain, and some still exist, for example the Druids Sheffield Friendly Society.

The Albion Lodge of the Ancient Order, however, was decidedly aristocratic, with the Duke of Leeds and Earl of Warwick as members and the Duke of Marlborough as patron. It was to that lodge that Marlborough's relative Winston Churchill was inducted at

What did druid gods look like? For the truly nutty, one should turn to Aylett Sammes. These appear to be his attempts to picture druidic deities based on Egyptian hieroglyphs

Blenheim on 15 August 1908: a photograph of the event is reproduced in Stuart Piggott's book *The Druids* (1968), and shows many of the members in white Father Christmas outfits with false beards, clearly not a totally serious event. (The beards caused a brief scare in 1911, when the Lodge feared that sharing them around might spread TB.)

There was and is rather more religion involved in some other groups, for example the Universal Bond of the Sons of Men, which was founded by George Watson Reid who, after flirtations with Buddhism, Islam and sun-worship, decided he was really Chief Druid. The Bond was notorious for inventing its own history, claiming that John Aubrey had revitalised a society founded in Oxford in 1245. Its actual date of origin was more likely 1915.

Neo-druid groups of a rather different kind arose later in the twentieth century. Many were neo-pagans, with varied belief systems, but mostly stressing veneration of Nature. Apparently some are still attempting to align their practices with ancient druidry, a hopeless task if it is to be done from the evidence, but perhaps conjecture will be as fruitful for them as it was for their eighteenth century equivalents.

The place of conjecture

A very recent archaeological find about a mile from Stonehenge was a canine tooth, 7000 years old, apparently from an Alsatian, one of the oldest domesticated animals ever discovered. Chemical analysis showed it wasn't local: in fact it had lived in Yorkshire as a puppy. The probability is that it had walked there with its owner. This adds to existing evidence suggesting that the Stonehenge area was a gathering place well before the monument was begun.

But what it is *not* is proof that the area was a site of ancient pilgrimage. Even if there were gatherings in the Stonehenge area 7000 years ago, they might have had another function, for example inter-tribal conferences.

And the dog might have been a stray, or its owner might have been a trader in high quality flints walking along the A303. Conjecture has its place: proof is something else.

An idealised druidic landscape, as imagined by Borlase

So, were there druids in the South-West?

From the historical evidence, as now understood

Quite probably. But as there is no reliable classical reference to druids in Britain other than their final retreat to Anglesey, which is described by Tacitus, who may himself not be entirely trustworthy, we cannot be certain even of that.

The archaeological evidence for druids

Quite simply, there is none. Archaeologists have been unable to identify any object as reliably associated with druidism. But nor is there any proof that there were no druids.

The West Country megaliths

If there were druids, did they have anything to do with the building of the West Country's megaliths? Almost certainly not, since the advent of radio-carbon dating and other archaeological advances leads us to believe that most of these were constructed between two and four thousand years before Caesar's time.

It is of course possible that some beliefs, such as transmigration of souls in which the druids were said to believe, might have been around when the megaliths were built, but even two thousand years is a long time for a belief system to stay unchanged. At Stonehenge, there is no evidence of any Iron Age activity, which suggests the monument was no longer relevant by the time of the druids.

This total uncertainty has not spoiled my own appreciation of the stone rows and circles of the West Country. I have visited as many of them as I could, especially those on Dartmoor and in West Penwith.

Usually there will be nobody else there, a very different experience from Stonehenge, and the sites are often in the midst of moorland far from the nearest road, so there is a great tranquillity. There is no point in trying to guess what rites went on there, or what the ancient people believed. You don't need to imagine a druid. Just appreciate the whole place for what it is, and what it means. To you. Now.

Extracts from two Classical texts

Julius Caesar, The Gallic War, Book 6

Throughout Gaul there are two classes of men of rank and hon-our. The common people are held almost as slaves, doing nothing on their own account, their opinion not consulted. Most of them, pressured by lack of money or the amount of tribute demanded or the injustice of their superiors, put themselves into servitude to the nobility, who have the same legal rights over them as owners over slaves.

Of the two classes of men of rank, one is that of druids, the other of knights. The druids are concerned with divine matters, they take care of public and private sacrifice and interpret religious ques-tions. A great many young men rush to them for education and hold them in great honour. It is they who make the decisions in almost all public and private disputes: whether a crime has been committed, or a killing, or there's a question of inheritance or a boundary dispute, they judge it and impose compensation or pun-ishments.

If an individual or a community ignores their judgement, they are excluded from the sacrifices: among them, that is the supreme punishment. Those so excluded are held to be impious and wicked, everyone avoids them and will not meet or talk with them in case they are themselves infected: if they later seek justice, they do not receive it, and they receive no honours.

For all these druids there is a single leader, who has the highest authority among them. When he dies, either the worthiest of those who remain succeeds him, or if there are many of equal excellence, they contest for supremacy by the votes of the druids, or even sometimes by force of arms.

At a certain time of the year they congregate in a sacred spot within the territory of the Carnutes, which is considered the centre of Gaul. To that place comes everyone from the whole country who has a dispute, and they accept the decisions and judgements of the assembly. It is thought that the training [*disciplina*, which could mean 'philosophical system'] originated in Britain and was then brought into Gaul, and nowadays those who are particularly keen to understand it generally head there for further education.

The druids usually steer clear of war, and do not pay military taxes like the rest. They are exempt from military service and from all compulsory public office. Tempted by these advantages, many young men turn to the druids of their own accord, and many are sent by their parents and relatives. It is said that they learn a great number of verses there by heart: some stay in that education for twenty years.

They do not think it proper to commit this oral learning to paper, though in almost all other matters, in public and private transactions, they make use of Greek script. This seems to me to have two reasons, that they don't want the training to be widely known, nor for those who learn to study to rely on writing, rather than memory: because it often happens that students who put reading first neglect diligence in thorough learning, and memory.

They especially wish to convince believers that souls do not perish, but after death they move from body to body, and they think this greatly increases valour, since fear of death is forgotten. Besides this they discuss with their students much about the stars and their movements, about the size of the universe and the earth, the nature of things [de rerum natura, perhaps a reference to Lucretius, implying an Epicurean philosophy], the immortality of the gods and their power.

The whole nation of the Gauls is devoted to religion, and for that reason those suffering severe illness or exposed to war or other dangers either sacrifice human victims or vow that they will, and they use the druids to conduct such sacrifices, because they believe that, unless the life of a man is delivered in return for the life of a man, the divine will of the immortal gods cannot be placated. In public life as well as private they have the same practice of sacrifice.

Others have images of immense size, whose limbs made of woven osiers they fill with living men: these they set on fire, and the men die in the conflagration.

They consider that the punishment of people who have been caught committing burglary, highway robbery or other crimes is preferable to the gods, but when there's no supply of those, they resort to sacrificing the innocent…

Pliny, Natural History: Mistletoe

Upon this occasion we must not omit to mention the admiration that is lavished upon this plant by the Gauls. The druids – for that is the name they give to their magicians – hold nothing more sacred than the mistletoe and the tree that bears it, supposing always that tree to be the robur [pedunculate oak]. Of itself the robur is selected by them to form whole groves, and they perform none of their religious rites without employing branches of it; so much so, that it is very probable that the priests themselves may have received their name from the Greek name for that tree. In fact, it is the notion with them that everything that grows on it has been sent immediately from heaven, and that the mistletoe upon it is a proof that the tree has been selected by God himself as an object of his especial favour.

The mistletoe, however, is but rarely found upon the robur; and when found, is gathered with rites replete with religious awe. This is done more particularly on the fifth day of the moon, the day which is the beginning of their months and years, as also of their ages, which, with them, are but thirty years. This day they select because the moon, though not yet in the middle of her course, has already considerable power and influence; and they call her by a name which signifies, in their language, the all-healing.

Having made all due preparation for the sacrifice and a banquet beneath the trees, they bring thither two white bulls, the horns of which are bound then for the first time. Clad in a white robe the priest ascends the tree, and cuts the mistletoe with a golden sickle, which is received by others in a white cloak. They then immolate the victims, offering up their prayers that God will render this gift of his propitious to those to whom he has so granted it. It is the belief with them that the mistletoe, taken in drink, will impart fecundity to all animals that are barren, and that it is an antidote for all poisons. Such are the religious feelings which we find entertained towards trifling objects among nearly all nations.

Pliny, Natural History, The druids of the Gallic provinces

The Gallic provinces, too, were pervaded by the magic art, and that even down to a period within memory; for it was the Emperor Tiberius that put down their druids, and all that tribe of wizards and physicians.

But why make further mention of these prohibitions, with reference to an art which has now crossed the very Ocean even, and has penetrated to the void recesses of Nature?

At the present day, struck with fascination, Britannia still cultivates this art, and that, with ceremonials so august, that she might almost seem to have been the first to communicate them to the people of Persia. To such a degree are nations throughout the whole world, totally different as they are and quite unknown to one another, in accord upon this one point!

Such being the fact, then, we cannot too highly appreciate the obligation that is due to the Roman people, for having put an end to those monstrous rites, in accordance with which, to murder a man was to do an act of the greatest devoutness, and to eat his flesh was to secure the highest blessings of health.

Other books you might find interesting

Ruth Scurr, *John Aubrey, My Own Life*

Ronald Hutton, *Blood and Mistletoe*

Stuart Piggott, *The Druids*

Stuart Piggott, *Ancient Britons and the Antiquarian Imagination*

Rosemary Sweet, *Antiquaries, The discovery of the past in eighteenth century Britain*

At the time of writing it is possible to find online the key works of Aubrey, Borlase, Stukeley, Rowlands, John Wood and Polwhele, as well as the classical authors.